Stitch POLDARK

Bring Poldark to Life With 6 Cross Stitch Charts

www.sewandso.co.uk

Contents

POLDARK

INTRODUCTION

Cornwall 1783 – a time of mining, seafaring, smuggling and social inequality... This land, this time, provides a stage for two unlikely lovers – Ross Poldark, an impoverished gentleman and army officer, recently returned from the American War of Independence, and Demelza Carne, a serving wench and feisty daughter of a drunk turned zealot. Ross and Demelza, destined for a life together in turbulent times.

Their story, and those in their orbit, was told by Winston Graham from 1945 to 1953 and continued by him in 1973 until 2002, during which time he wrote twelve novels for the series. Graham had a great love of Cornwall and this shows in his stories, which contain a wealth of detail about the Cornish people and life in this rugged south-west peninsula of England. The BBC first adapted the novels for television in 1975, and 2015 saw the story being given new life and shown again on the BBC to great acclaim.

The new cast of Poldark has Aidan Turner and Eleanor Tomlinson in the lead roles and this re-invigorated version has attracted a whole new audience of devoted fans. The ravishing scenery of Cornwall is as much part of this new series as the memorable characters. And there's drama aplenty too, with a fascinating collection of characters, striving to survive amid riot and revolution and where infection and inequality are daily companions.

The beautiful cross stitch scenes charted in this book have been created for you to capture a little of this land, this time and these people, to bring these characters and this scenery to life. Whether it's Ross riding along the dramatic Cornish coastline or Demelza in contemplative mood, this collection is perfect for Poldark fans.

Poldark Country

Ross Poldark, the eponymous hero of the evocative Winston Graham novels, is as rugged as the Cornish coast near his land. Like the jagged rocks that guard Nampara Cove, he stands firm ready to face all that life might throw at him.

You Will Need

- 14-count Aida (or 28-count evenweave) 51cm x 38cm (20in x 15in)
- DMC stranded cotton (floss) as listed in chart key
- Tapestry needle size 24–26

STITCH COUNT

196 stitches wide
x 124 stitches high

DESIGN SIZE ON 14-COUNT

35.5cm x 22.5cm (14in x 9in)

CHARTS LAYOUT

1	2	3
4	5	6

Stitching the Design

1 Prepare for work. If desired, you can colour photocopy and enlarge the charts (for your own personal use), and tape them together, ready for sewing. Mark the centre point of your fabric and the centre stitch on the chart. Mount your fabric in an embroidery frame if desired.

2 Start stitching from the centre of the fabric and chart, working over one block of Aida or over two threads of evenweave fabric. Use two strands of thread throughout for all full cross stitches.

3 When stitching is complete display your work as desired. If required, see Techniques: Making Up.

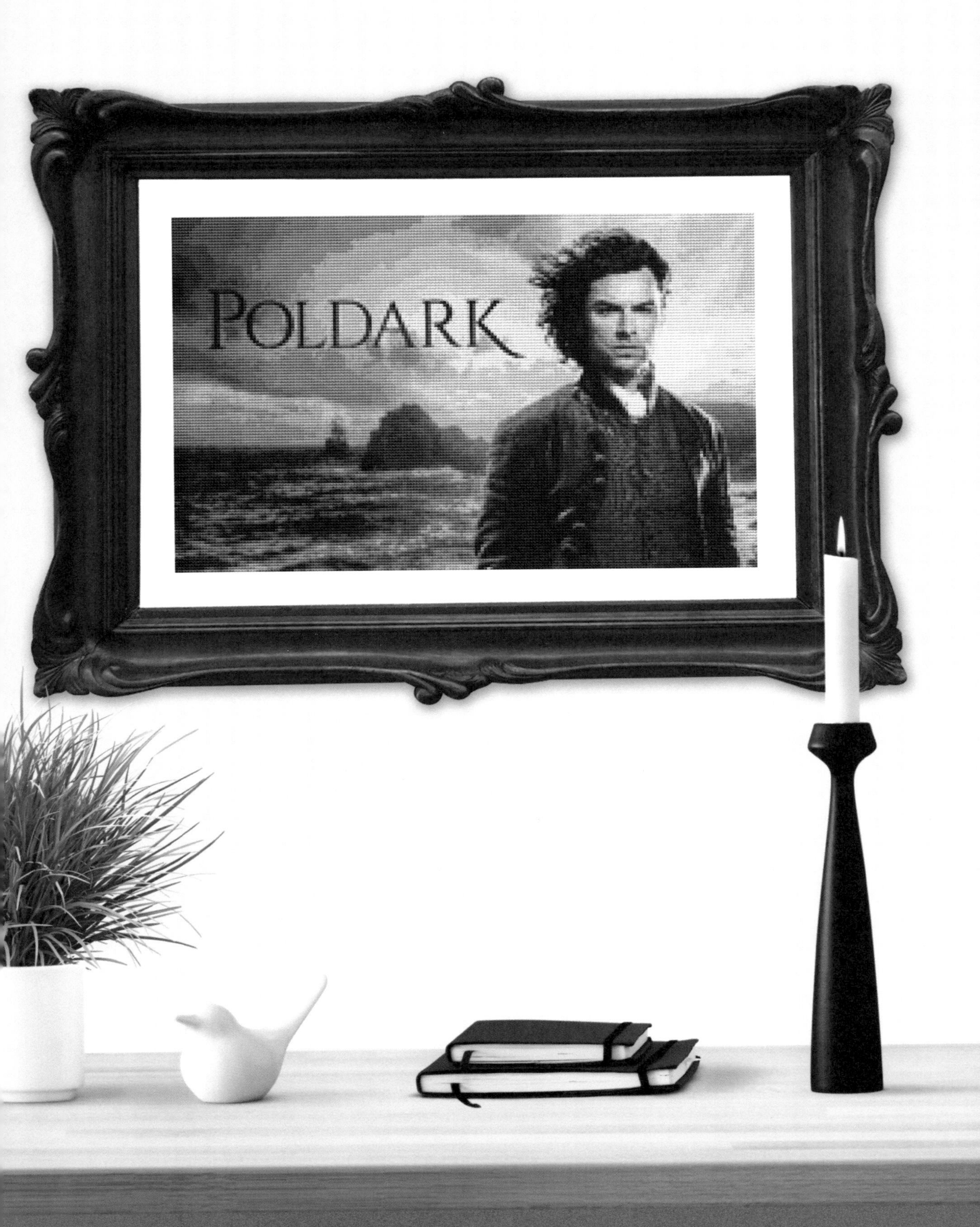
POLDARK

Chart 1

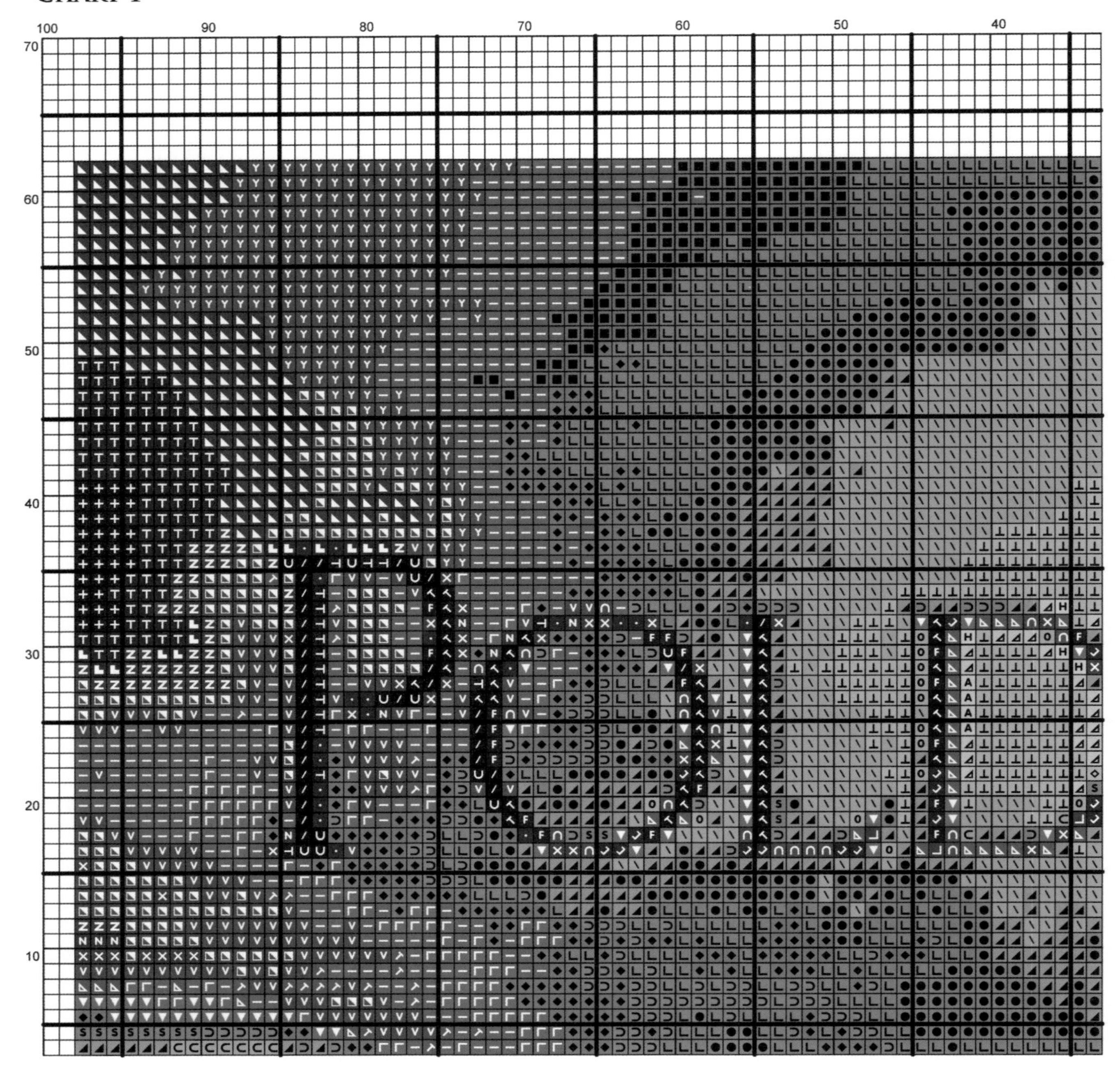

POLDARK COUNTRY

Cross stitch
DMC stranded cotton (2 strands)

DMC	Symbol	DMC	Symbol	DMC	Symbol	DMC	Symbol	DMC	Symbol	DMC	Symbol	DMC	Symbol
154	↖	436	1	647	—	839	·	951	H	3371	U	3860	X
224	▽	437	⧓	648	●	840	∩	3022	⋏	3771	¬	3863	◺
310	/	452	L	677	↩	842	◢	3023	◆	3782	⊃	3864	S
317	◣	543	◿	712	P	890	+	3024	\	3790	N	3865	○
318	■	640	V	746	⊙	930	T	3031	⊣	3823	◪	3866	A
400	✓	642	┌	754	★	934	=	3033	⊥	3828	▼	Ecru	□
402	J	645	Z	761	⊢	945	◇	3072	▬	3856	⊂		
414	Y	646	◩	780	┘	950	O	3362	▙	3857	F		

Chart 2

Chart 3

POLDARK COUNTRY

Cross stitch
DMC stranded cotton (2 strands)

154	436	647	839	951	3371	3860
224	437	648	840	3022	3771	3863
310	452	677	842	3023	3782	3864
317	543	712	890	3024	3790	3865
318	640	746	930	3031	3823	3866
400	642	754	934	3033	3828	Ecru
402	645	761	945	3072	3856	
414	646	780	950	3362	3857	

Chart 4

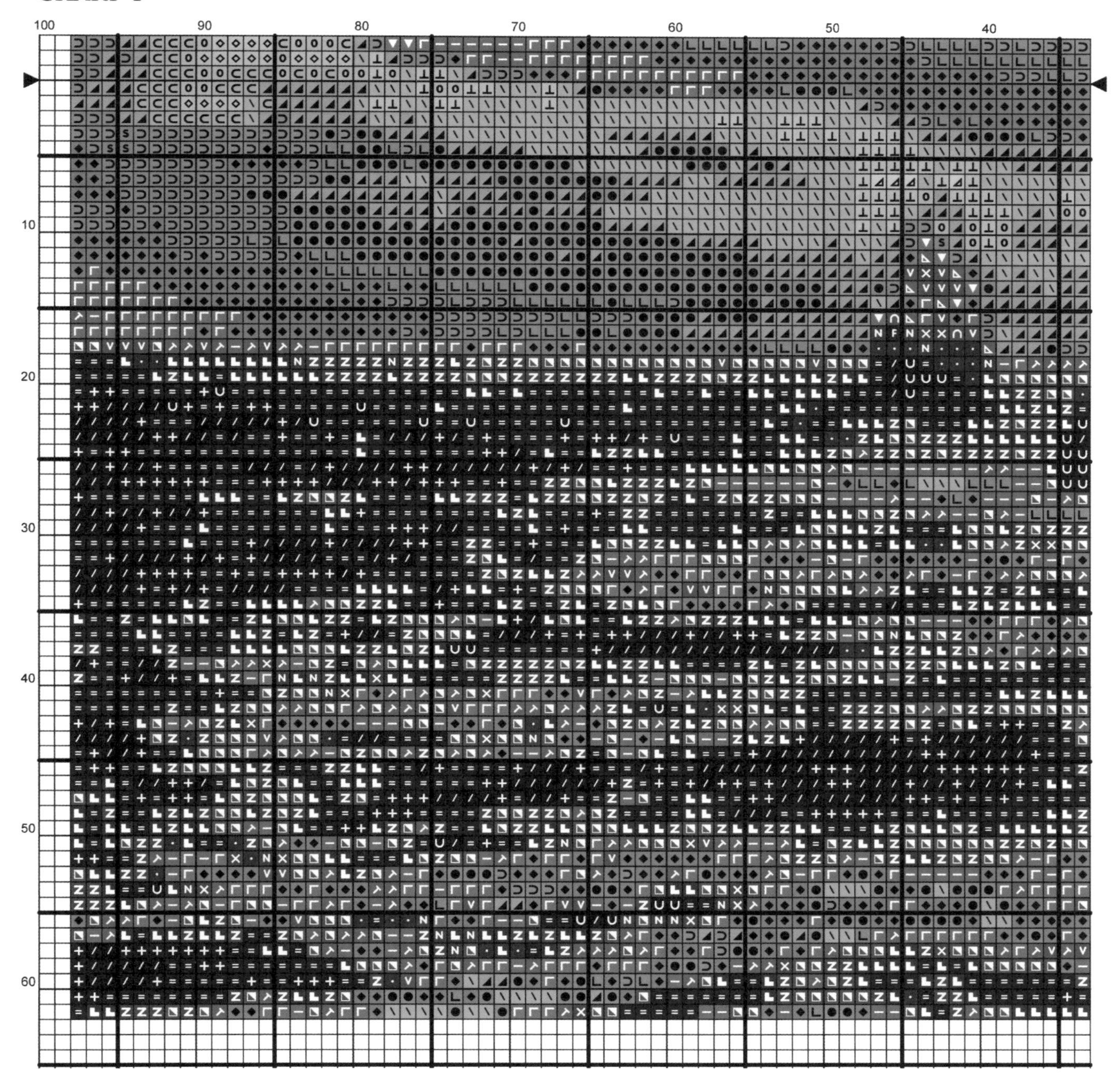

Chart 5

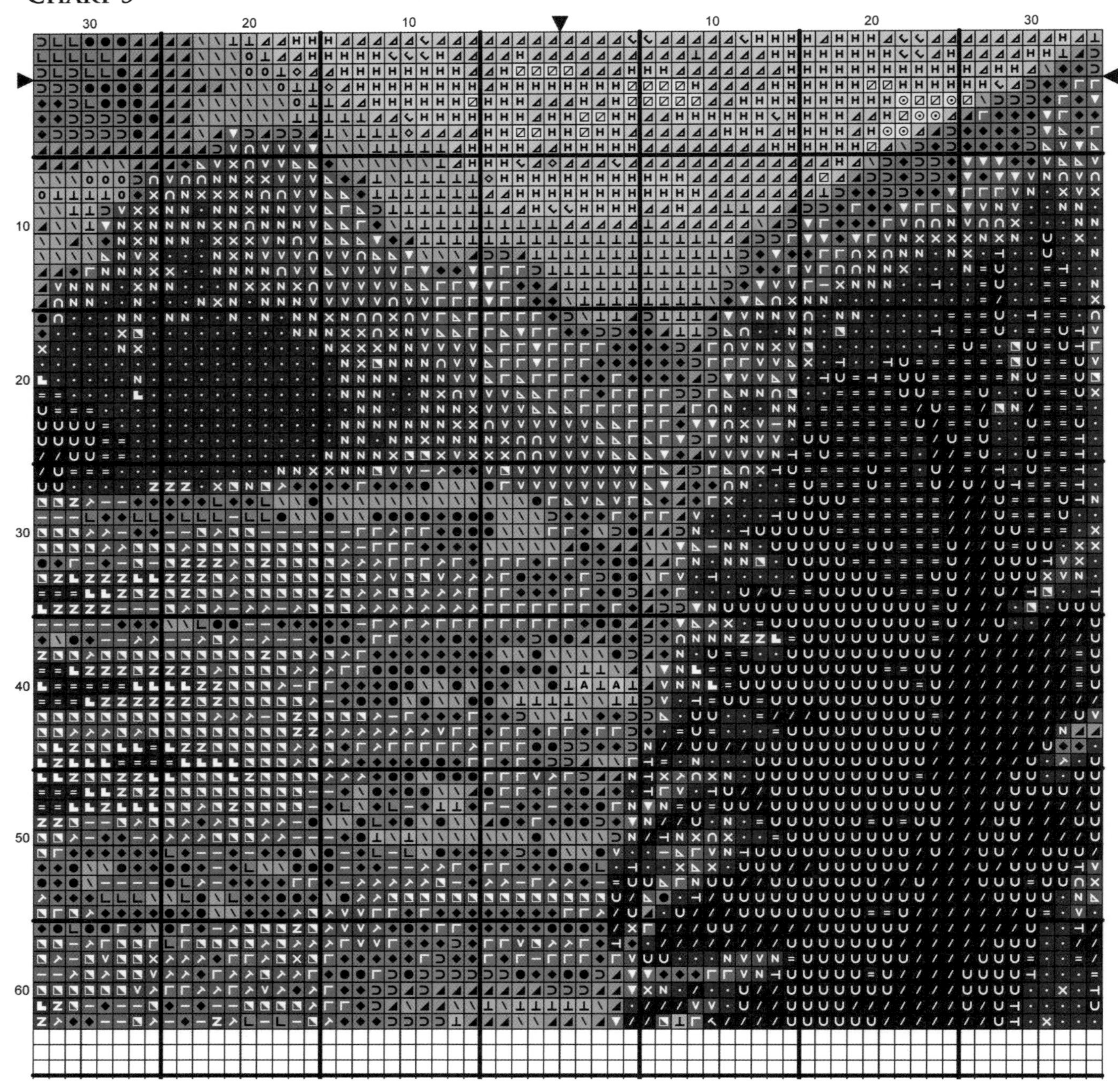

POLDARK COUNTRY

Cross stitch
DMC stranded cotton (2 strands)

DMC	Symbol	DMC	Symbol	DMC	Symbol	DMC	Symbol	DMC	Symbol	DMC	Symbol	DMC	Symbol
154	↖	436	1	647	—	839	·	951	H	3371	U	3860	X
224	▽	437	⋈	648	●	840	∩	3022	⅄	3771	¬	3863	◣
310	/	452	L	677	↩	842	◢	3023	◆	3782	⊃	3864	S
317	◣	543	◿	712	P	890	+	3024	\	3790	N	3865	O
318	■	640	V	746	⊙	930	T	3031	⊣	3823	▨	3866	A
400	✓	642	┌	754	★	934	=	3033	⊥	3828	▼	Ecru	□
402	J	645	Z	761	⊢	945	◇	3072	▬	3856	C		
414	Y	646	◪	780	┘	950	O	3362	▙	3857	F		

Chart 6

Fortunes May Change

The sea that pounds the craggy coastline of more than 400 miles was the lifeblood of Cornwall in the eighteenth century, vital for fishing, trade, and covert smuggling. Seafaring ventures though were high-risk and could make or break a man. No wonder then that harbours were places of intense business discussions, and intrigue.

You Will Need

- 14-count Aida (or 28-count evenweave) 48cm x 38cm (19in x 15in)
- DMC stranded cotton (floss) as listed in chart key – some colours need more than one skein
- Tapestry needle size 24–26

STITCH COUNT

182 stitches wide x 121 stitches high

DESIGN SIZE ON 14-COUNT

33cm x 22cm (13in x 8⅝in)

Stitching the Design

1 Prepare for work. If desired, you can colour photocopy and enlarge the charts (for your own personal use), and tape them together, ready for sewing. Mark the centre point of your fabric and the centre stitch on the chart. Mount your fabric in an embroidery frame if desired.

2 Start stitching from the centre of the fabric and chart, working over one block of Aida or over two threads of evenweave fabric. Use two strands of thread throughout for all full cross stitches.

3 When stitching is complete display your work as desired. If required, see Techniques: Making Up.

Chart 1

FORTUNES MAY CHANGE

Cross stitch / DMC stranded cotton (2 strands)

DMC	Symbol
168	T
169	◆
310	\
316	D
317	V
318	┘
413	◇
414	■
415	Z
451	✓
452	◢
453	X
535	L
610	<
640	P
642	↗
644	—
646	▙
647	<
648	⊙
762	U
801	J
838	⊥
839	N
840	○
841	★
842	▽
927	C
935	◺
938	∩
939	Y
3011	+
3021	▼
3022	◣
3032	⊃
3033	□
3041	⋈
3363	H
3364	●
3721	W
3756 (2 skeins)	┐
3772	⊢
3782	0
3787	S
3790	A
3799	⊣
3858	F
3861	◢
3862	3
3863	1
3864	/
3866	>
B5200 (3 skeins)	•

CHART 2
10
20
30
40
50
60
70
80
90

Wild Flower

A wild child of nature, Demelza finds comfort in the lush fields and the rambling beauty of the Cornish countryside. When she is not hard at work in the kitchen, often doing the work of lazy Jud and Prudie too, she escapes to the flower-filled meadow to dream of a better life, accompanied by her ever-faithful dog, Garrick.

You Will Need

- 14-count Aida (or 28-count evenweave) 51cm x 40.5cm (20in x 16in)
- DMC stranded cotton (floss) as listed in chart key – one colour needs more than one skein
- Tapestry needle size 24–26

STITCH COUNT

196 stitches wide x 131 stitches high

DESIGN SIZE ON 14-COUNT

35.5cm x 24cm (14in x 9⅜in)

CHARTS LAYOUT

1	2	3
4	5	6

Stitching the Design

1 Prepare for work. If desired, you can colour photocopy and enlarge the charts (for your own personal use), and tape them together, ready for sewing. Mark the centre point of your fabric and the centre stitch on the chart. Mount your fabric in an embroidery frame if desired.

2 Start stitching from the centre of the fabric and chart, working over one block of Aida or over two threads of evenweave fabric. Use two strands of thread throughout for all full cross stitches.

3 When stitching is complete display your work as desired. If required, see Techniques: Making Up.

CHART 1

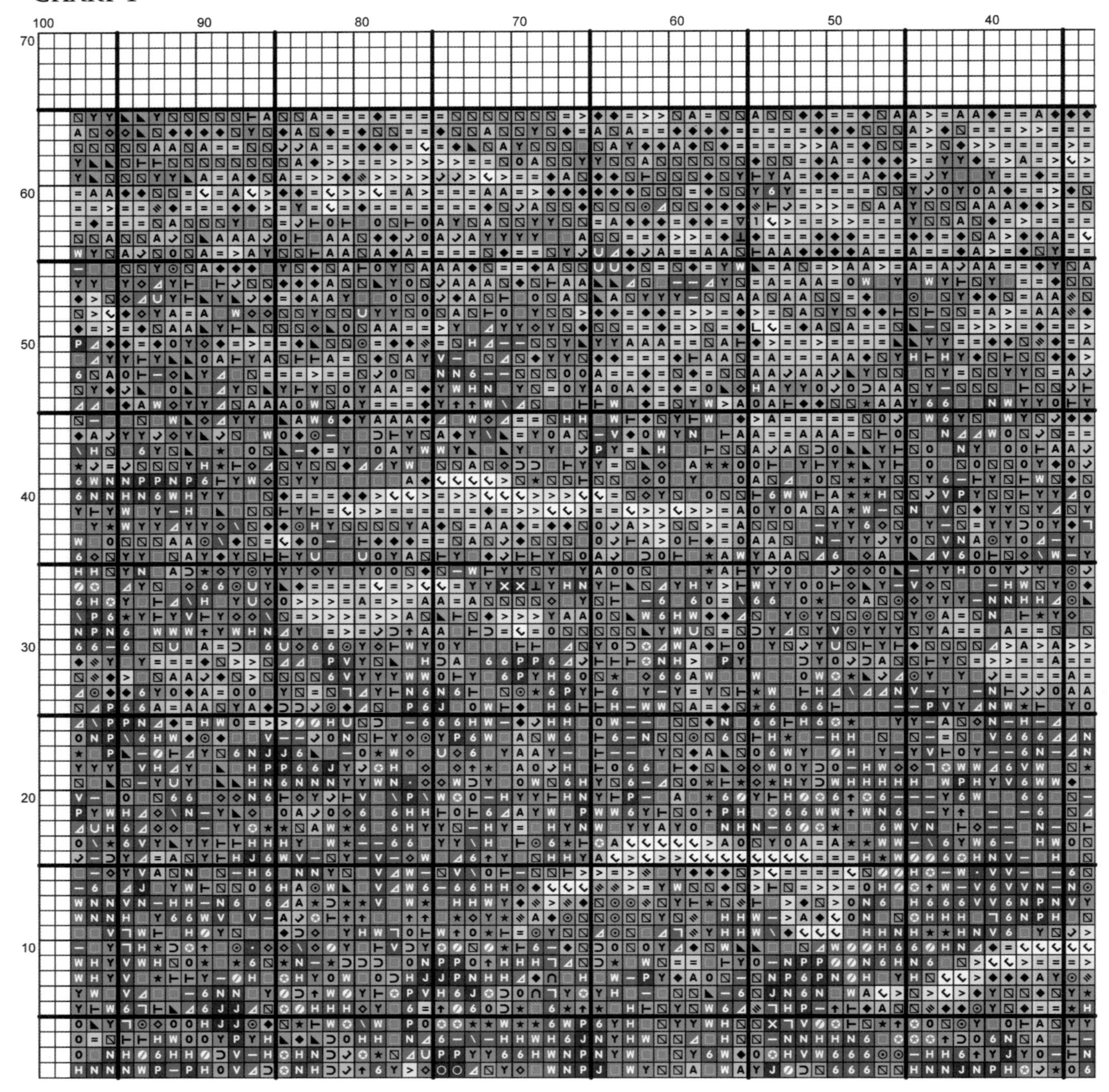

WILD FLOWER

Cross stitch / DMC stranded cotton (2 strands)

DMC	Symbol
156	⊥
165	⊃
166	✪
307	
340	
341	▽
369	A
370	\
415	/
433	S
469	N
470	6
471	■
472	0
524	⊙
581	H
611	•
613	◇
640	V
642	U
644 (2 skeins)	⧅
648	∩
712	>
730	P
733	W
734	★
762	1
792	⇒
793	⋌
809	⊂
822	=
840	◺
841	◿
907	⊘
928	⫽
936	J
3013	Y
3022	¬
3031	♥
3033	◆
3045	←
3046	◣
3047	✓
3347	—
3348	⊢
3746	+
3747	⋲
3756	L
3781	○
3787	✕
3807	◑
3819	↑
3839	⊕
3865	

Chart 2

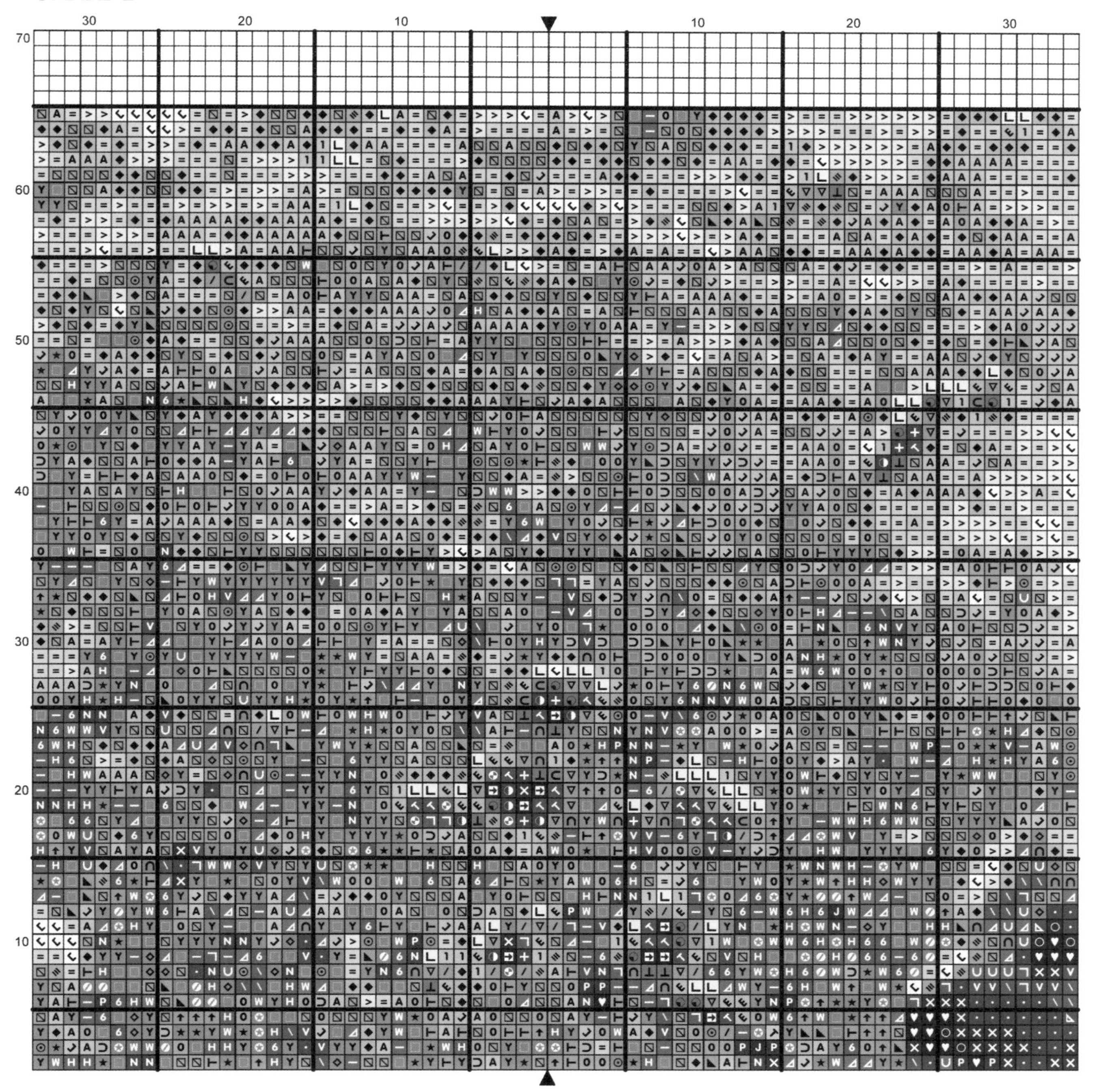

CHART 3

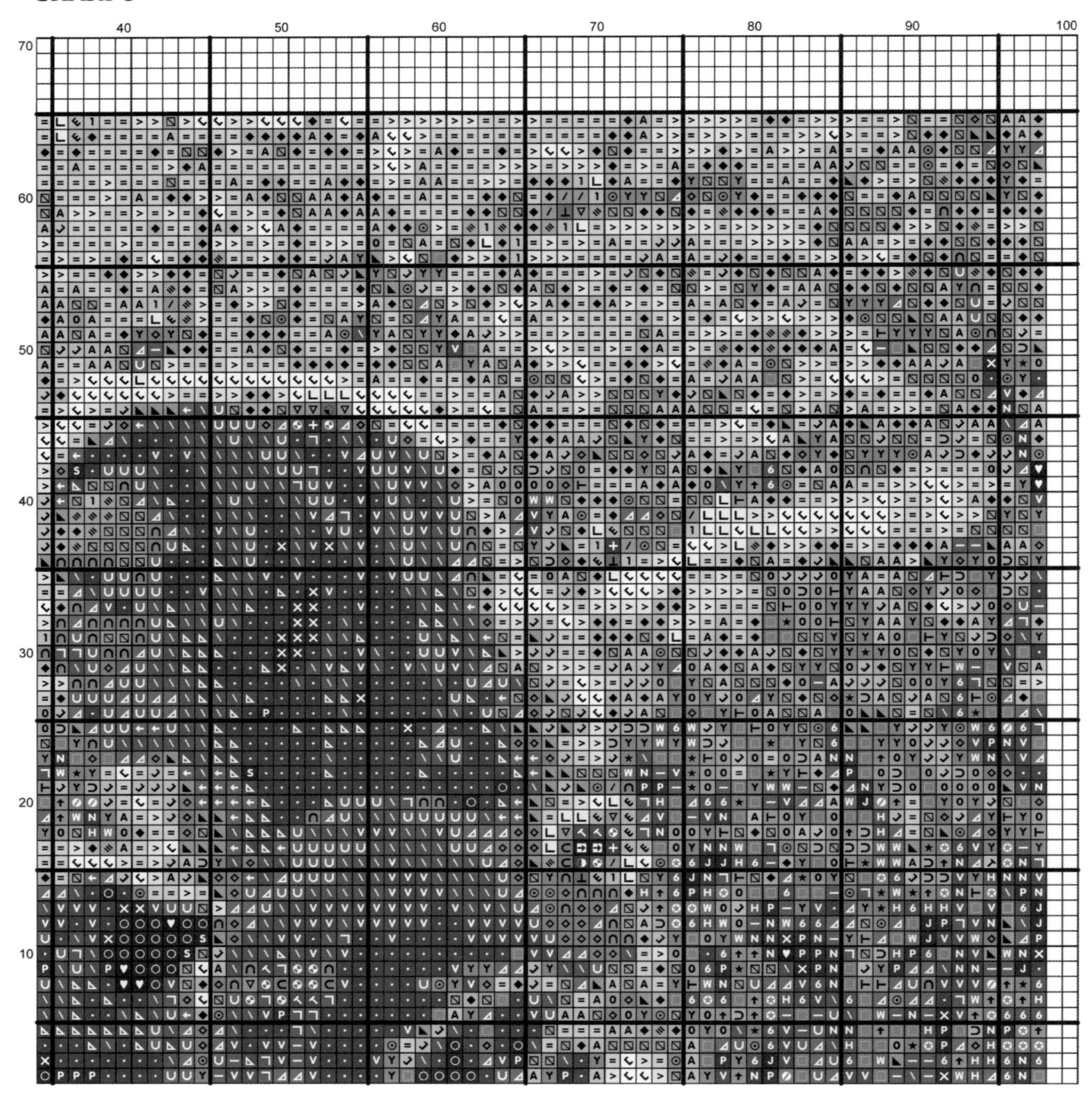

WILD FLOWER

Cross stitch / DMC stranded cotton (2 strands)

DMC	Symbol	DMC	Symbol	DMC	Symbol	DMC	Symbol	DMC	Symbol	DMC	Symbol	DMC	Symbol
156	⊥	415	/	611	•	730	P	840	◣	3033	◆	3756	L
165	⊃	433	S	613	◇	733	W	841	◿	3045	←	3781	○
166	✪	469	N	640	V	734	★	907	⊘	3046	◣	3787	×
307	↗	470	6	642	U	762	1	928	⫽	3047	↲	3807	◑
340	◔	471	blank	644 (2 skeins)	⊠	792	⇨	936	J	3347	—	3819	↑
341	▽	472	0	648	∩	793	↖	3013	Y	3348	⊢	3839	✇
369	A	524	⊙	712	>	809	⊂	3022	¬	3746	+	3865	↩
370	\	581	H			822	=	3031	♥ (solid square)	3747	⇐		

CHART 4

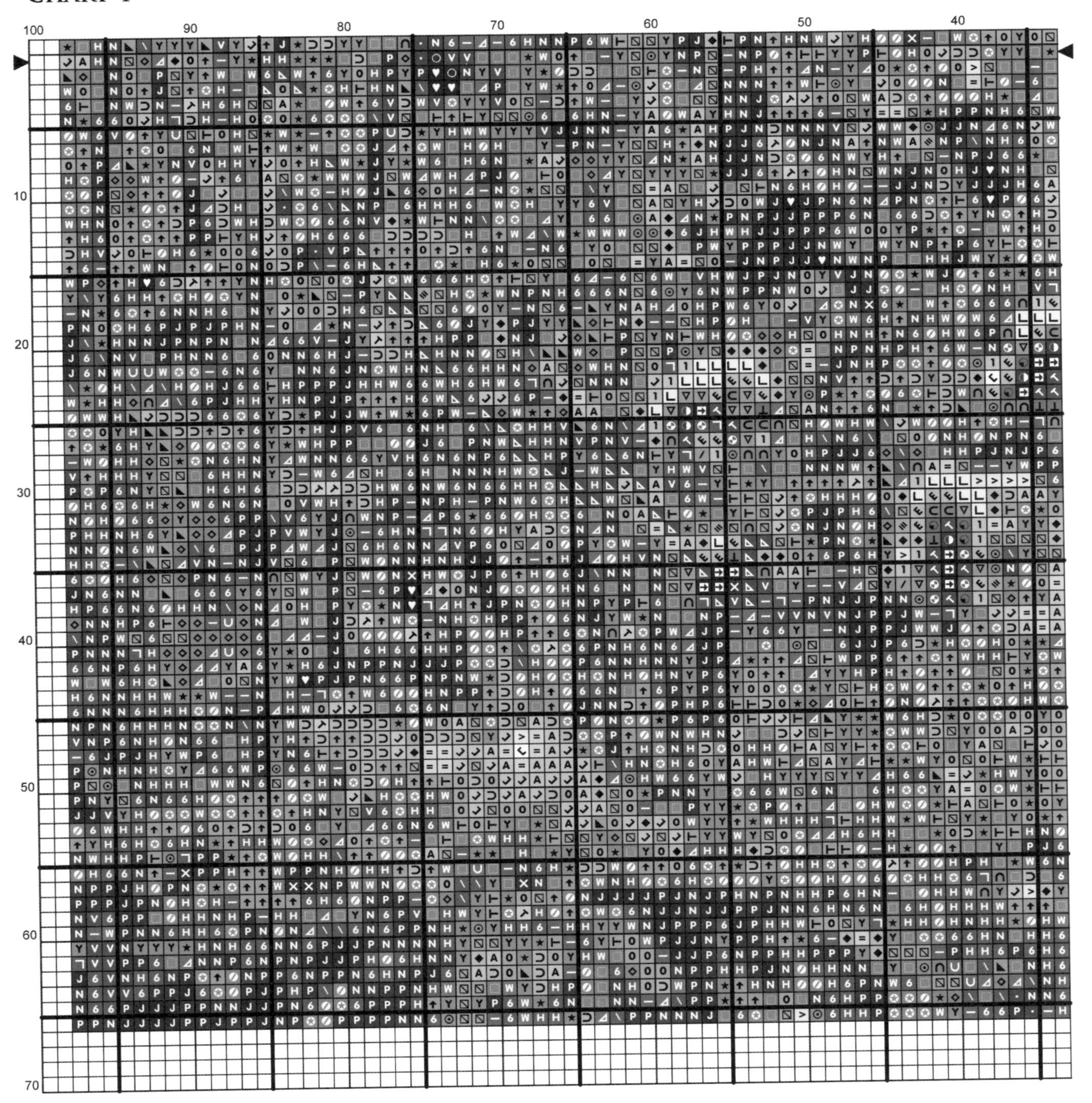

Chart 5

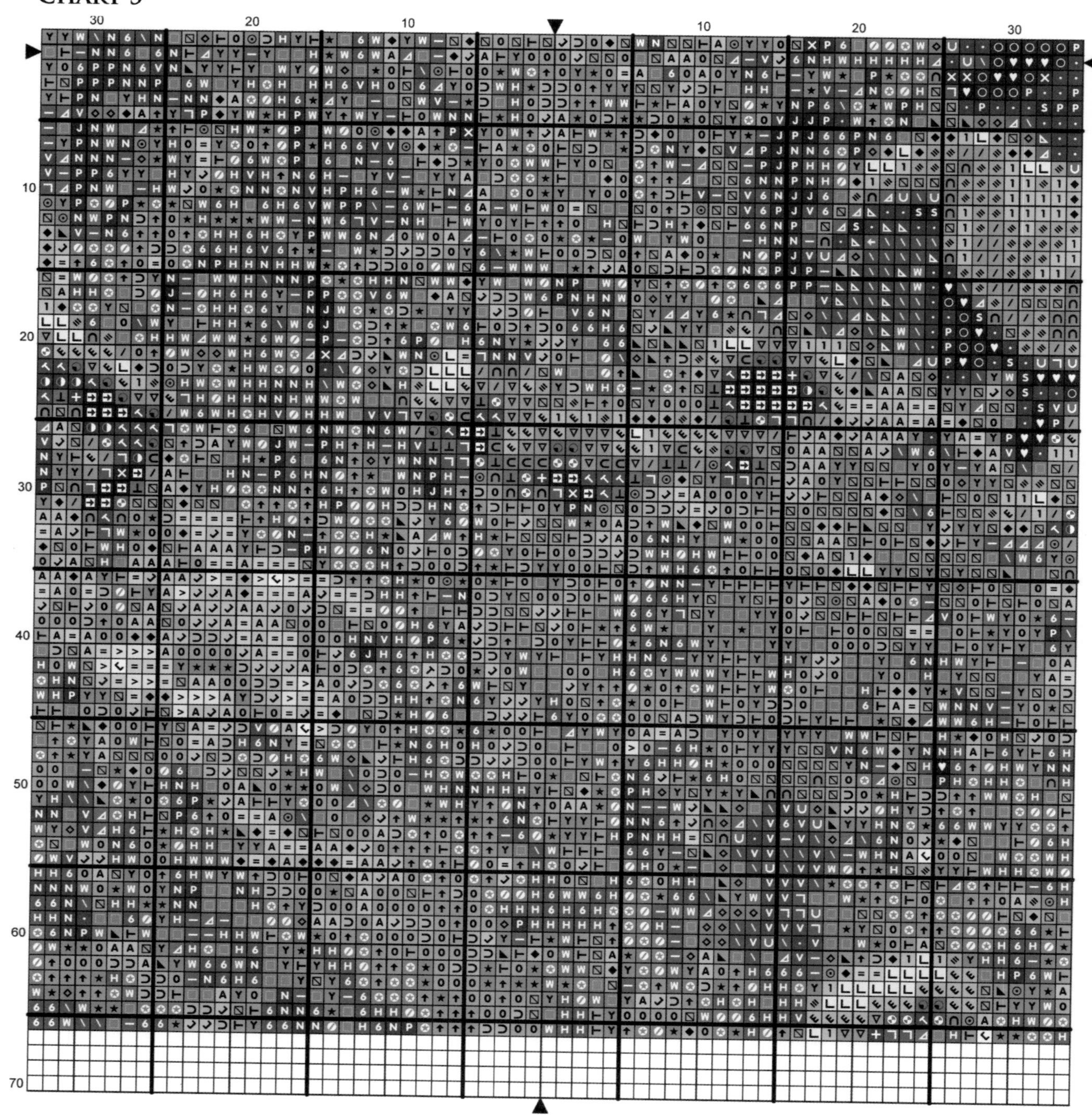

WILD FLOWER

Cross stitch / DMC stranded cotton (2 strands)

DMC	Symbol	DMC	Symbol	DMC	Symbol	DMC	Symbol	DMC	Symbol	DMC	Symbol	DMC	Symbol
156	⊥	415	/	611	·	730	P	840	◺	3033	◆	3756	L
165	⊃	433	S	613	◇	733	W	841	◿	3045	←	3781	○
166	✪	469	N	640	V	734	★	907	⊘	3046	◣	3787	×
307	↗	470	6	642	U	762	1	928	⸗	3047	✓	3807	◐
340	◒	471		644 (2 skeins)	⧄	792	➔	936	J	3347	—	3819	↑
341	▽	472	O	648	∩	793	↖	3013	Y	3348	⊢	3839	⊗
369	A	524	⊙	712	>	809	C	3022	┐	3746	+	3865	↙
370	\	581	H			822	=	3031	♥	3747	⪡		

Chart 6

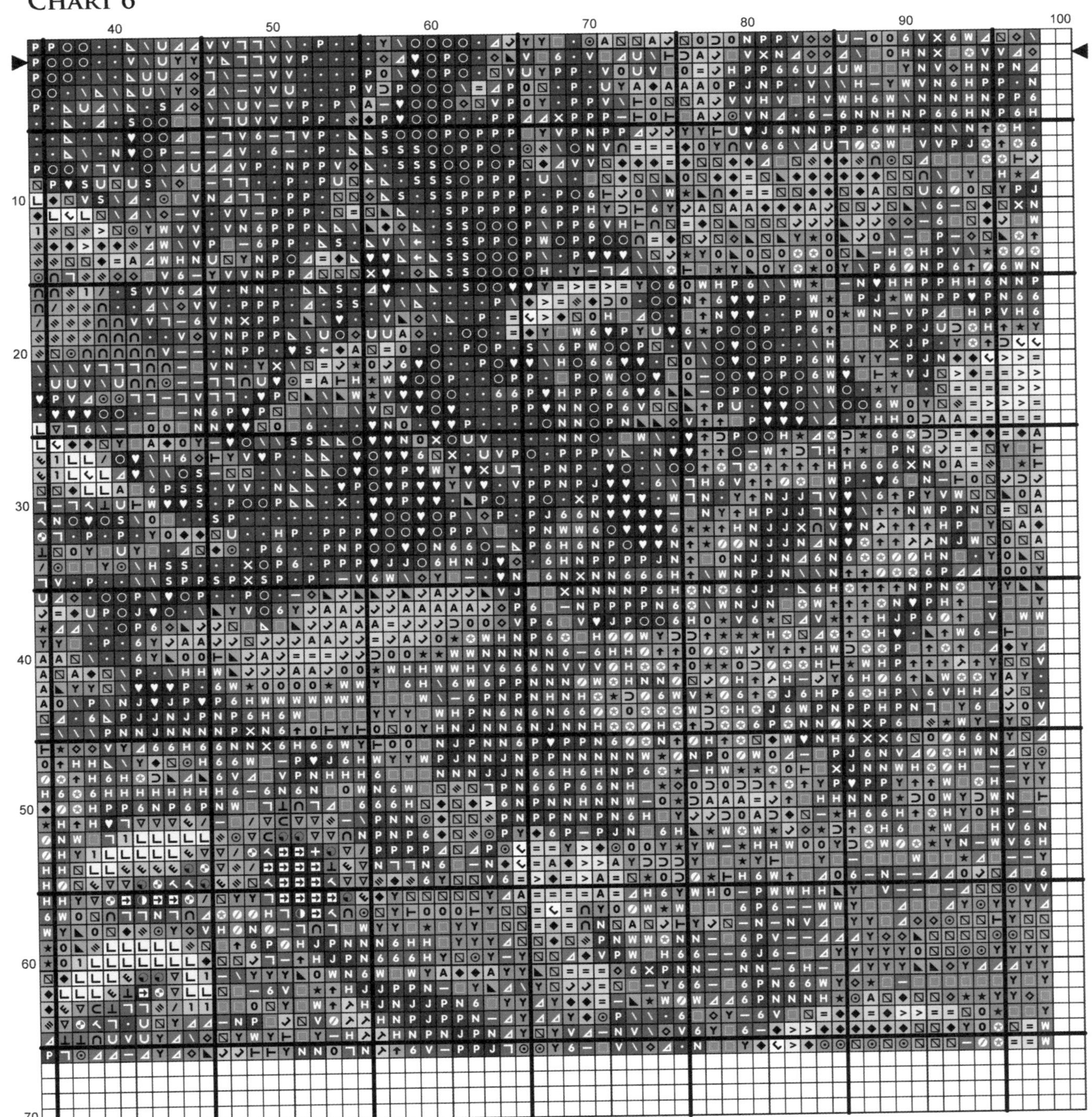

Nampara Bound

Riding through stunning Cornish scenery, Ross spends many hours journeying from his home at Nampara to his copper mine Wheal Leisure, and to the trade towns in the area, including Bodmin and Truro. Horse-back was the quickest way for a gentleman to travel across rolling hills and along miles of coastline, especially an impoverished one who couldn't afford a carriage.

You Will Need

- 14-count Aida (or 28-count evenweave) 51cm x 40.5cm (20in x 16in)
- DMC stranded cotton (floss) as listed in chart key – some colours need more than one skein
- Tapestry needle size 24–26

STITCH COUNT

196 stitches wide x 131 stitches high

DESIGN SIZE ON 14-COUNT

35.5cm x 24cm (14in x 9⅜in)

Stitching the Design

1 Prepare for work. If desired, you can colour photocopy and enlarge the charts (for your own personal use), and tape them together, ready for sewing. Mark the centre point of your fabric and the centre stitch on the chart. Mount your fabric in an embroidery frame if desired.

2 Start stitching from the centre of the fabric and chart, working over one block of Aida or over two threads of evenweave fabric. Use two strands of thread throughout for all full cross stitches.

3 When stitching is complete display your work as desired. If required, see Techniques: Making Up.

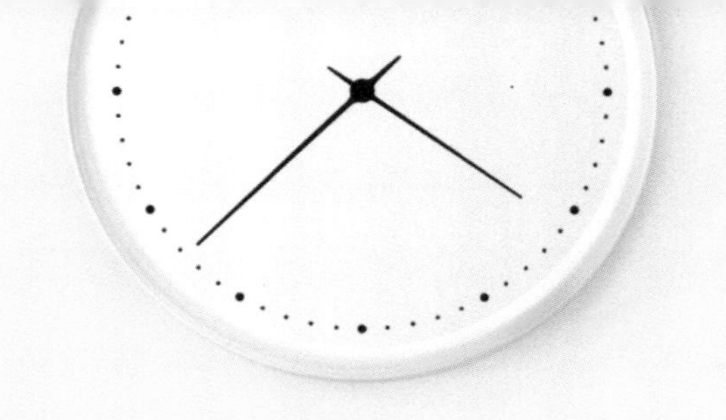

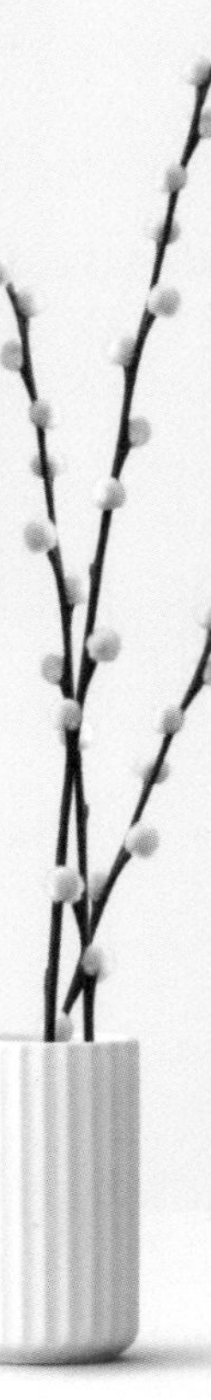

Chart 1

NAMPARA BOUND

Cross stitch / DMC stranded cotton (2 strands)

DMC	Symbol
162	■
310	–
317	◇
318	O
370	=
371	✓
372	◆
413	1
415	★
471	◺
472	L
524	⋈
535	Z
611	<
640	⌐
644	┤
646	X
647	⊃
648	◣
732	P
734	●
775 (4 skeins)	•
839	▽

DMC	Symbol
898	/
930	^
934	◿
935	T
939	∩
3012	U
3013	H
3021	C
3023	▼
3052	Y
3053	→
3072	□
3371	✓
3753	S
3756 (3 skeins)	○
3787	+
3790	N
3799	┘
3841	⊥
3860	V
B5200 (3 skeins)	\

Chart 2

Love of My Life

When Demelza is gravely ill with putrid fever Ross is distraught, having already lost his sweet little daughter, Julia. When Elizabeth asks Ross what she can do to help, he tells her to pray to God that he doesn't lose the love of his life too. His prayer is answered and his red-haired love survives.

You Will Need

- 14-count Aida (or 28-count evenweave) 51cm x 40.5cm (20in x 16in)
- DMC stranded cotton (floss) as listed in chart key – one colour needs more than one skein
- Tapestry needle size 24–26

STITCH COUNT

196 stitches wide x 131 stitches high

DESIGN SIZE ON 14-COUNT

35.5cm x 24cm (14in x 9⅜in)

CHARTS LAYOUT

1	2	3
4	5	6

Stitching the Design

1 Prepare for work. If desired, you can colour photocopy and enlarge the charts (for your own personal use), and tape them together, ready for sewing. Mark the centre point of your fabric and the centre stitch on the chart. Mount your fabric in an embroidery frame if desired.

2 Start stitching from the centre of the fabric and chart, working over one block of Aida or over two threads of evenweave fabric. Use two strands of thread throughout for all full cross stitches.

3 When stitching is complete display your work as desired. If required, see Techniques: Making Up.

CHART 1

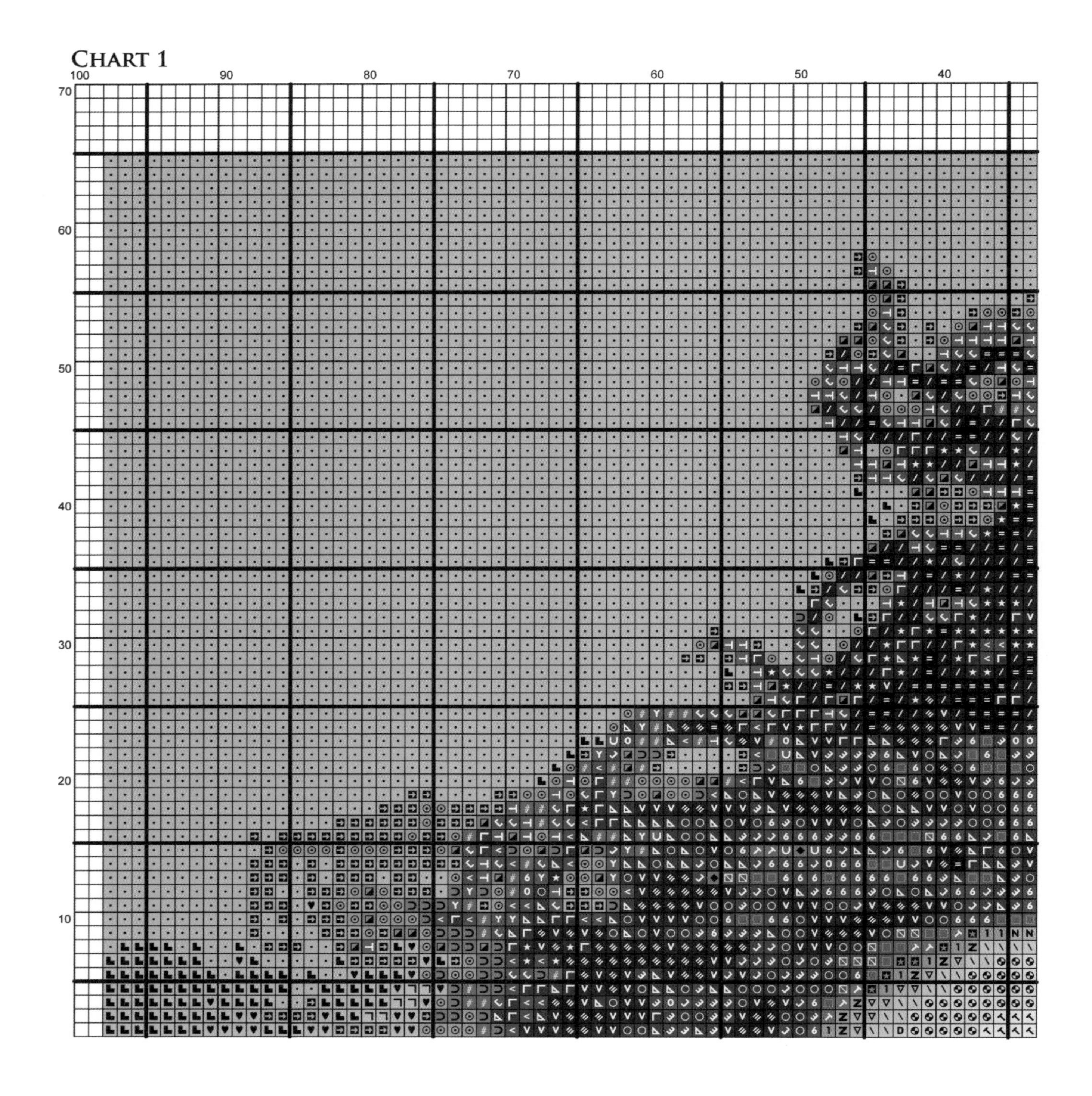

LOVE OF MY LIFE

Cross stitch
DMC stranded cotton (2 strands)

DMC	Symbol
152	◇
159	⊙
167	W
223	—
300	V
310	=
316	⊂
318	⊃
372	■
436	↑
451	Y
472	◢
535	┌
543	\
611	↘
640	O
642	∩
644	Z
646	<
647	#
648	⬇
712	⋌
738	⊥
775	✪
778	P
822	D
828	▙
840	6
841	↗
842	1
844	★
931	↙
938	⫽
950	N
3023	←
3032	◆
3033	▽
3325	➔
3747	♥
3753	┐
3755	◪
3761 (5 skeins)	•
3772	⧄
3774	◔
3782	⧆
3790	◺
3799	/
3839	⊣
3858	○
3860	↘
3861	U
3863	□
3865	◒
Ecru	◐

CHART 2

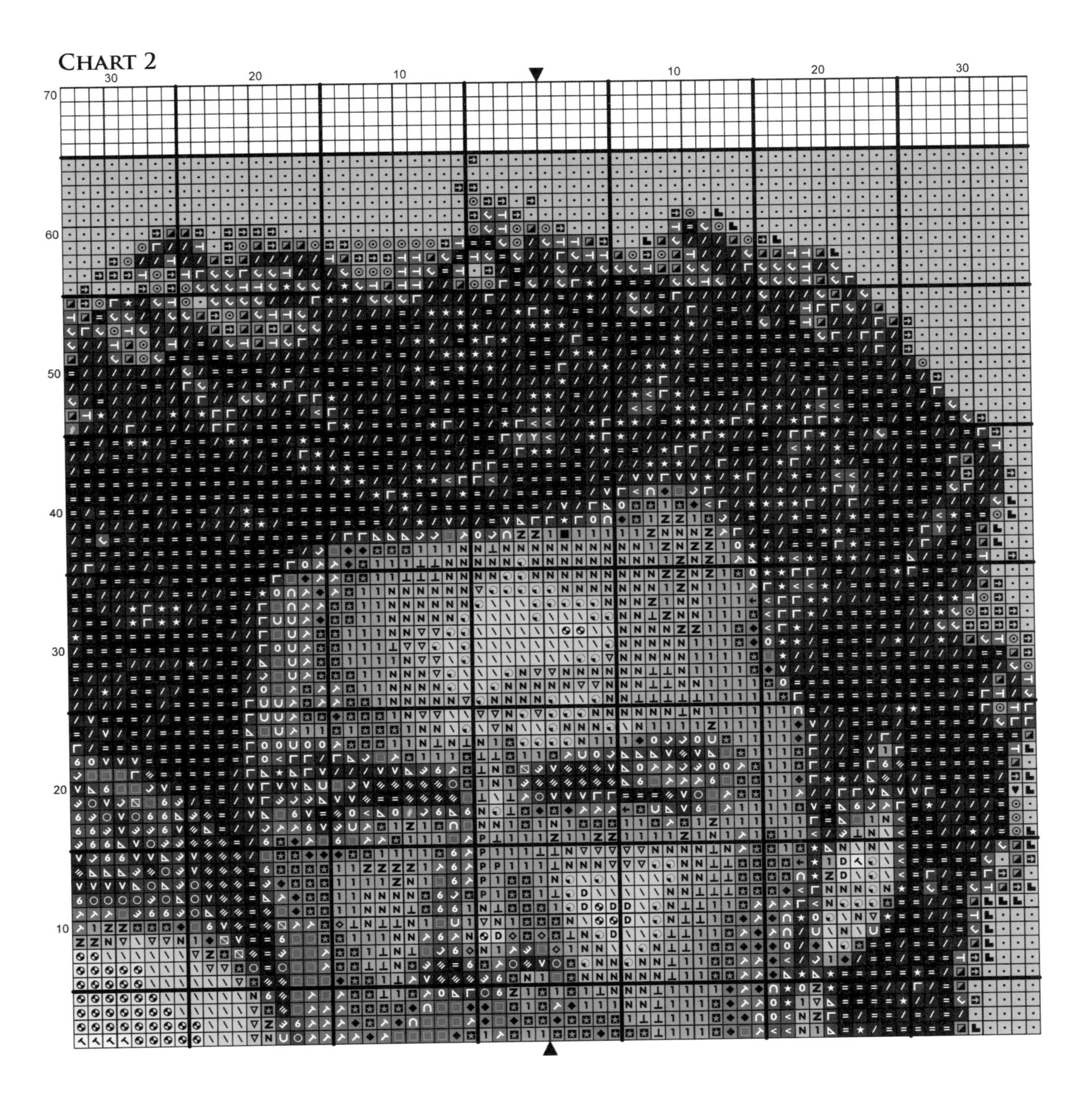

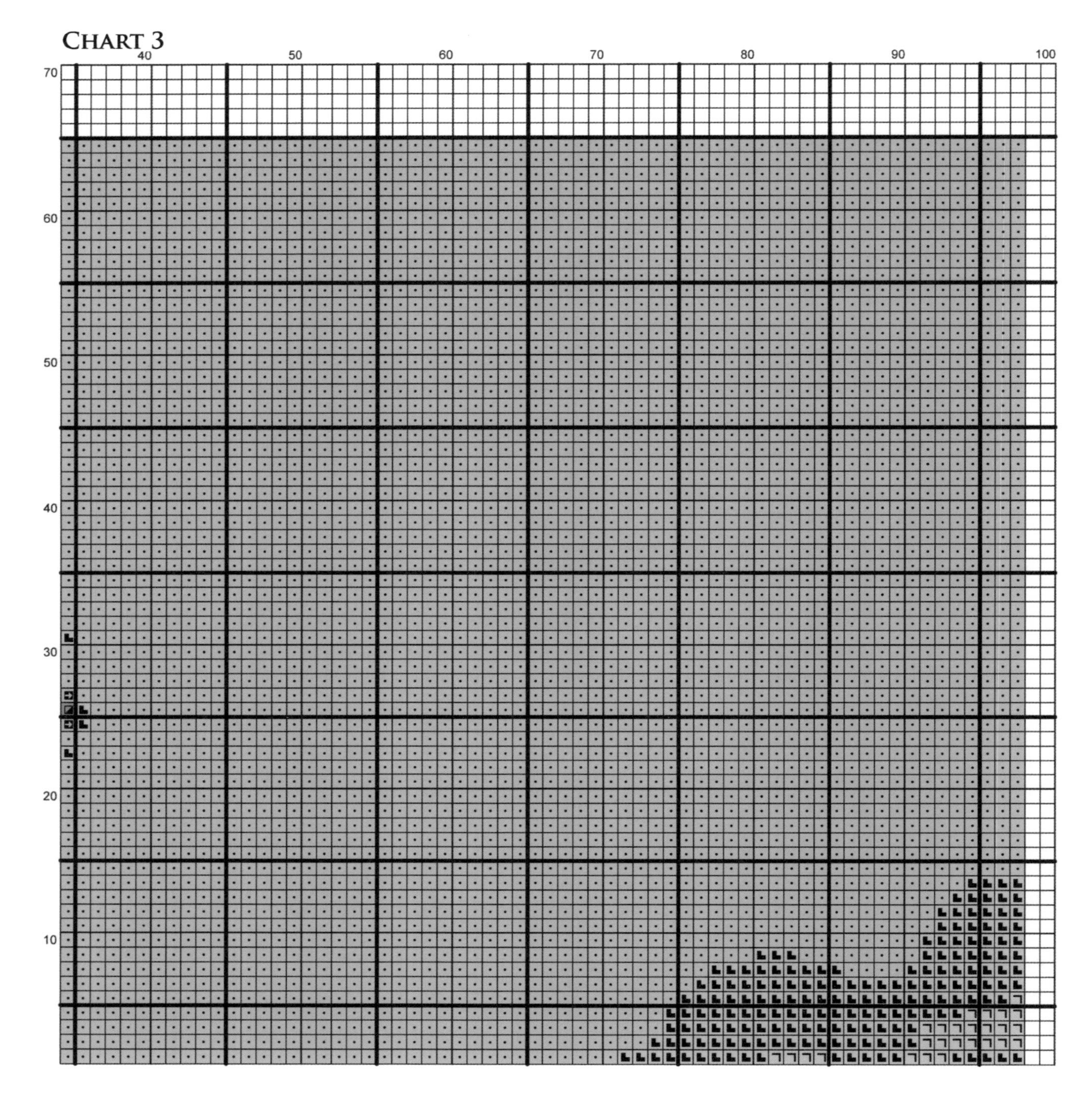

LOVE OF MY LIFE

Cross stitch
DMC stranded cotton (2 strands)

DMC	Symbol	DMC	Symbol	DMC	Symbol	DMC	Symbol	DMC	Symbol	DMC	Symbol	DMC	Symbol
152	◇	372	■	642	∩	778	P	938	⫽	3755	◪	3839	⊤
159	⊙	436	↑	644	Z	822	D	950	N	3761 (5 skeins)	•	3858	○
167	W	451	Y	646	<	828	▙	3023	←	3772	⧅	3860	≥
223	—	472	◢	647	#	840	6	3032	◆	3774	◔	3861	U
300	V	535	Γ	648	⇩	841	^	3033	▽	3782	★	3863	□
310	=	543	\	712	⋌	842	1	3325	⇨	3790	◺	3865	◒
316	⊂	611	✓	738	⊥	844	★	3747	♥	3799	/	Ecru	◕
318	⊃	640	O	775	✪	931	<	3753	⌝				

CHART 4

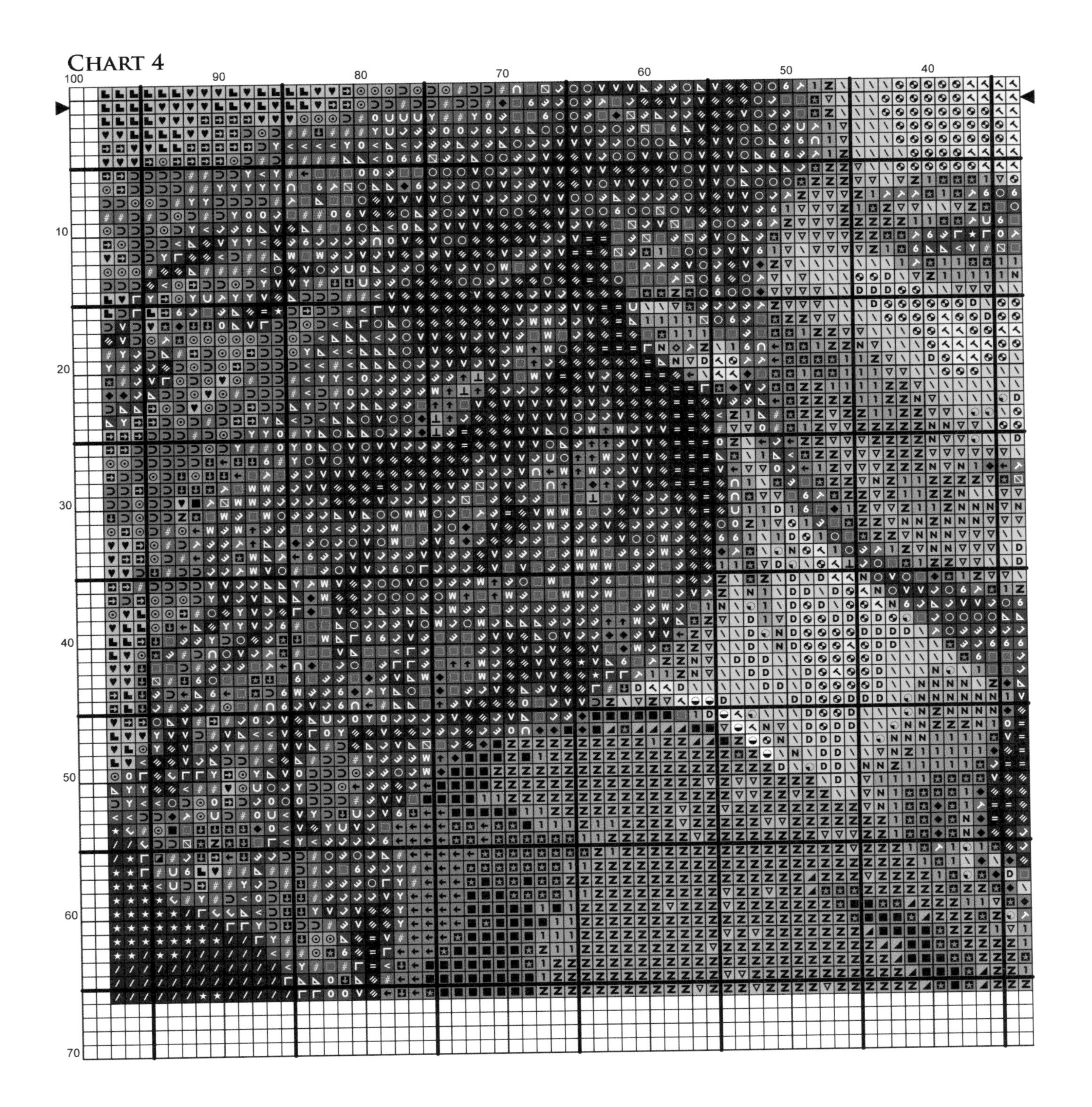

LOVE OF MY LIFE

Cross stitch

DMC stranded cotton (2 strands)

DMC	Symbol
152	◇
159	⊙
167	W
223	—
300	V
310	=
316	⊂
318	⊃
372	■
436	↑
451	Y
472	◢
535	Γ
543	\
611	✓
640	O
642	∩
644	Z
646	<
647	#
648	⬇
712	⛏
738	⊥
775	✪
778	P
822	D
828	▙
840	6
841	↗
842	1
844	★
931	↙
938	⫽
950	N
3023	←
3032	◆
3033	▽
3325	⇨
3747	♥
3753	⌐
3755	◪
3761 (5 skeins)	•
3772	⧄
3774	◐
3782	⊠
3790	◣
3799	/
3839	⊣
3858	○
3860	↪
3861	U
3863	□
3865	◒
Ecru	⊕

Chart 6

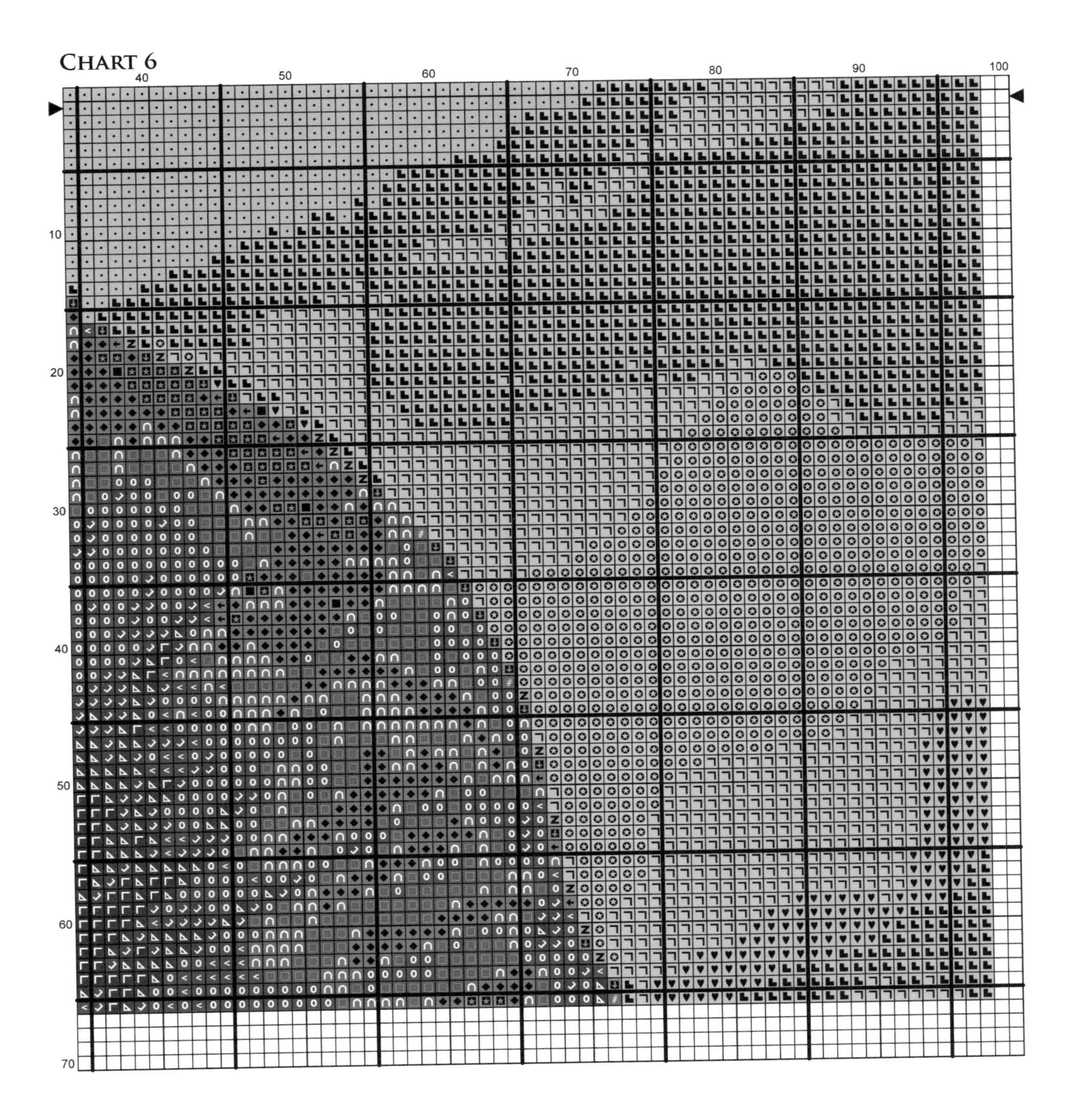

The Road Not Taken

Returning from the war in America, Ross is desperate to see his sweetheart, Elizabeth. However, he is devastated to find that she is engaged to his cousin, Francis, soon to be married and lost to him forever – a sad homecoming indeed. He thinks he will never recover from the blow, and then Demelza comes into his life...

You Will Need

- 14-count Aida (or 28-count evenweave) 48cm x 38cm (19in x 15in)
- DMC stranded cotton (floss) as listed in chart key – some colours need more than one skein
- Tapestry needle size 24–26

STITCH COUNT

182 stitches wide x 121 stitches high

DESIGN SIZE ON 14-COUNT

33cm x 22cm (13in x 8⅝in)

Stitching the Design

1 Prepare for work. If desired, you can colour photocopy and enlarge the charts (for your own personal use), and tape them together, ready for sewing. Mark the centre point of your fabric and the centre stitch on the chart. Mount your fabric in an embroidery frame if desired.

2 Start stitching from the centre of the fabric and chart, working over one block of Aida or over two threads of evenweave fabric. Use two strands of thread throughout for all full cross stitches.

3 When stitching is complete display your work as desired. If required, see Techniques: Making Up.

CHART 1

THE ROAD NOT TAKEN

Cross stitch
DMC stranded cotton
(2 strands)

DMC	Symbol
166	J
167	○
221	\
310	A
355	⋖
451	F
470	V
502	⅄
535	U
581	Y
610	∩
613	⊂
640	◆
644	◪
646	▽
647	H
648	V
712	★
733	⋈
746	P
814	⌐
815	⊙
831	⋲
841	⊢
907	◔
924	⊥
928	◢

DMC	Symbol
935	+
937	Z
938	◣
939 (2 skeins)	/
3011	X
3021	S
3022	N
3024	⧄
3033	⋋
3042	↓
3072	◣
3371	✓
3768	◐
3772	1
3781	⌐
3782	<
3787	■
3799	⊃
3813	◇
3857	L
3860	T
3863	=
3864	—
3865 (2 skeins)	•
ecru	0

CHART 2

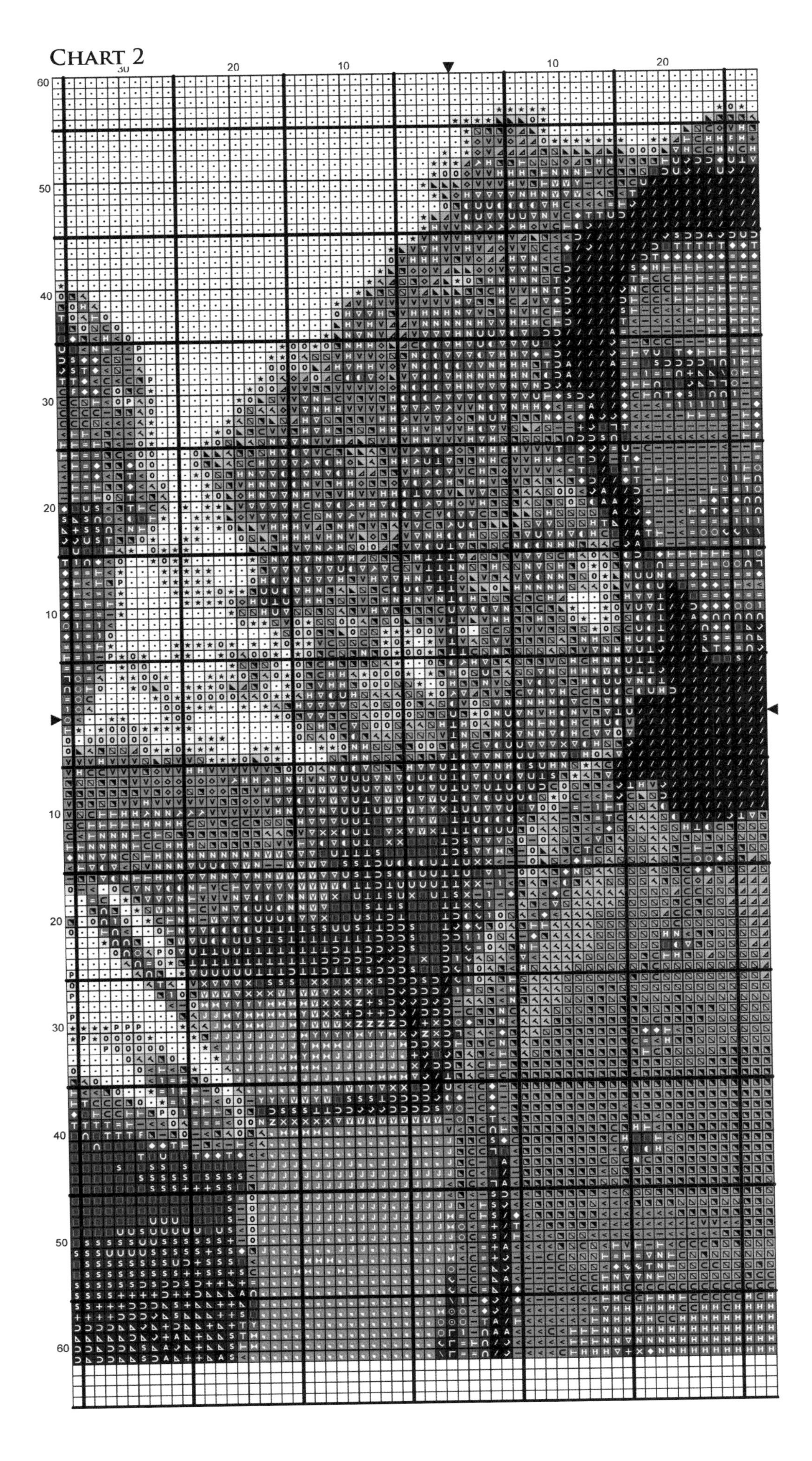

CHART 3

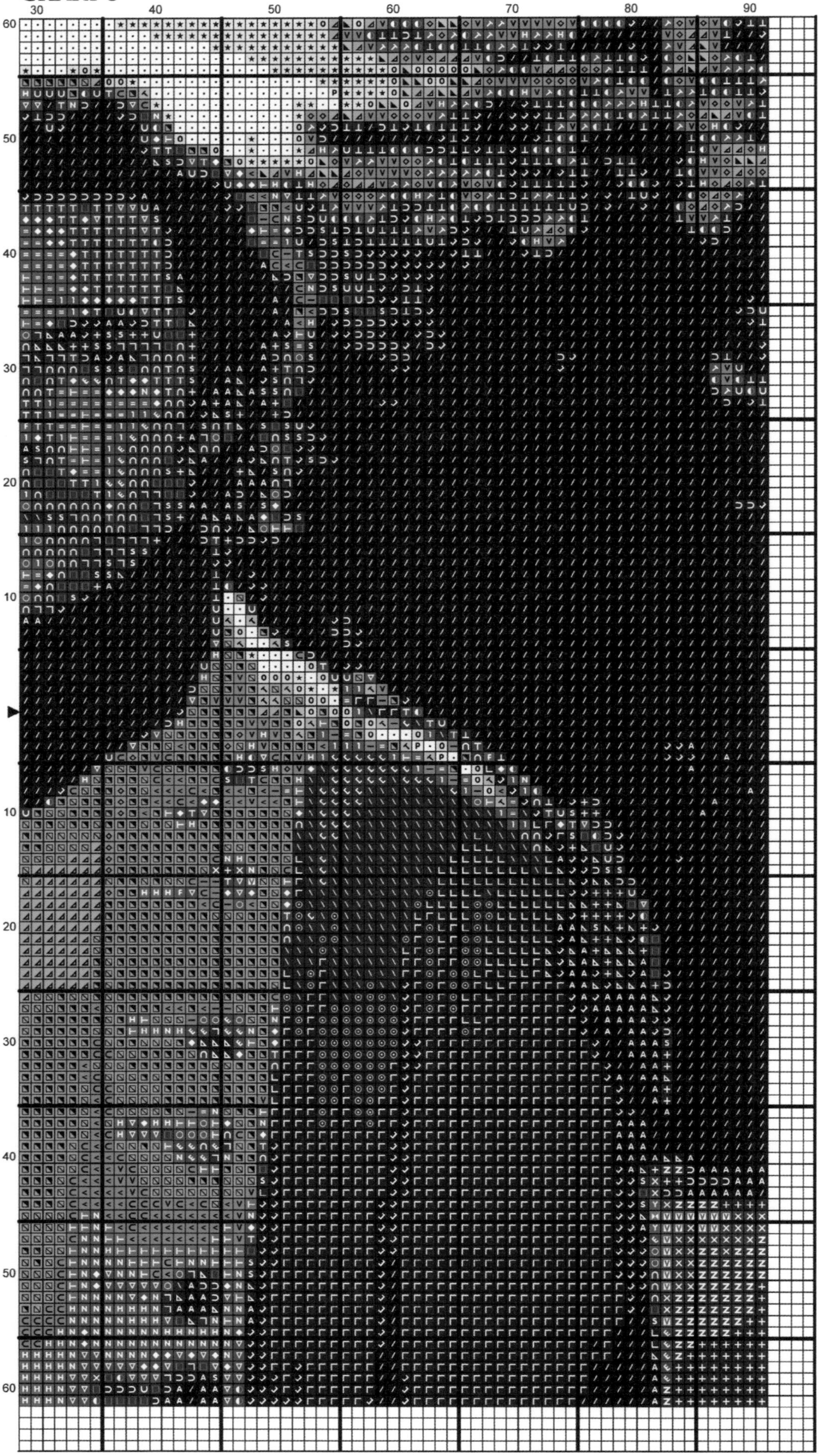

THE ROAD NOT TAKEN

Cross stitch
DMC stranded cotton
(2 strands)

DMC	DMC
166	935
167	937
221	938
310	939 (2 skeins)
355	3011
451	3021
470	3022
502	3024
535	3033
581	3042
610	3072
613	3371
640	3768
644	3772
646	3781
647	3782
648	3787
712	3799
733	3813
746	3857
814	3860
815	3863
831	3864
841	3865 (2 skeins)
907	ecru
924	
928	

MATERIALS AND EQUIPMENT

The following section gives advice on the materials and equipment you will need to stitch the charts in this book.

FABRICS

Fabrics used for counted cross stitch are woven so they have the same number of threads or blocks to 2.5cm (1in), both horizontally and vertically. The two main fabric types used are blockweaves, such as Aida, and evenweaves, such as linen.

Aida fabric is woven in blocks and is available in many colours and counts – 8, 11, 14, 16, 18 and 20 blocks to 2.5cm (1in). When stitching on Aida, one block on the fabric corresponds to one square on the chart. Each cross stitch is worked over one block.

Evenweave fabrics are woven singly, are made from various fibres and are available in many different colours and counts. When stitching on evenweave, each cross stitch is usually worked over two threads of the fabric.

THREADS

The most commonly used thread for counted embroidery is stranded cotton (floss) which is a six-stranded thread that can be bought by the skein in hundreds of colours with ranges made by DMC, Anchor and Madeira. The projects in this book use DMC threads.

EQUIPMENT

Very little equipment is needed for cross stitch embroidery and the following basics are all you need to get you started.

Needles

Use blunt tapestry needles for counted cross stitch. The commonest sizes used are 24 and 26 but the size depends on your project and personal preference. Avoid leaving a needle in the fabric unless it is gold plated or it may cause marks.

Scissors

Use dressmaker's shears for cutting fabric and a small, sharp pair of pointed scissors for cutting embroidery threads.

Frames and hoops

These are not essential but if you use one, choose one large enough to hold the complete design, to avoid marking the fabric and flattening stitches.

TECHNIQUES

This section will provide you with all the techniques you need to stitch the designs, so for the best results read through the next few pages before you begin stitching.

USING THE CHARTS

The designs in this book are worked from colour charts with symbols. Each square, both occupied and unoccupied, represents one block of Aida or two threads of linen. Each occupied square equals one cross stitch. Arrows at the sides of the charts allow you to find the centre easily. For your own personal use you could photocopy the charts in colour (and enlarge them too if you wish), and then stick the parts together to show the complete design.

CALCULATING THE DESIGN SIZE

Each project gives the stitch count and finished design size if worked on 14-count Aida (or 28-count evenweave) but if you plan to work the design on a different count you will need to be able to calculate the finished size. To do this, take the number of stitches in the design and divide this by the fabric count number, e.g., 140 stitches x 140 stitches ÷ by 14-count = a design size of 10in x l0in (25.5cm x 25.5cm). Remember that working on evenweave usually means working over two threads not one, so divide the fabric count by 2 before you start calculating for linen.

PREPARING THE FABRIC

The sizes given with the charts are for the finished design size only, therefore you will need to add at least 7.5cm (3in) to both measurements when cutting embroidery fabric, to allow enough fabric around the edges for working and for making up later. Before you begin stitching, press your embroidery fabric if necessary and trim the selvedge or any rough edges. Work from the middle of the fabric and middle of the chart to ensure that your design is centred on the fabric. Find the middle of the fabric by folding it in four and pressing lightly. Mark the folds with tailor's chalk or with lines of tacking (basting) following a fabric thread. When working with linen, prepare as described above but also sew a narrow hem around all raw edges to preserve them for finishing later.

STARTING AND FINISHING

Unless indicated otherwise, begin stitching in the middle of a design to ensure an adequate margin for making up. Start and finish stitching neatly and avoid knots that create lump.

Knotless loop start

This start can be used with an even number of strands, i.e., 2, 4 or 6. To stitch with two strands, begin with one strand about 80cm (30in). Double the thread and thread the needle with the two ends. Put the needle up through the fabric from the wrong side, where you intend to begin stitching, leaving the loop at the back (see Fig 1). Form a half cross stitch, put the needle back through the fabric and through the waiting loop to anchor the stitch.

Fig 1 Knotless loop start

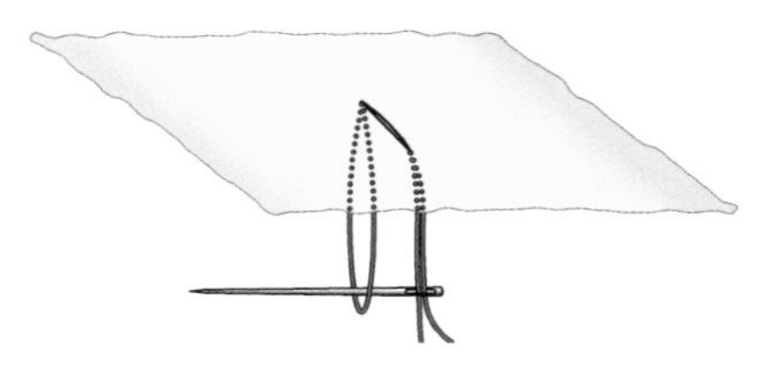

Away waste knot start

Start this way if using an odd number of strands. Thread the needle with the number of strands required and then knot the end. Insert the needle into the right side of the fabric, away from where you wish to begin stitching (see Fig 2). Stitch towards the knot and cut it off when the threads are anchored. Alternatively, snip off the knot, thread a needle and work under a few stitches to anchor the thread.

Fig 2 Away waste knot start

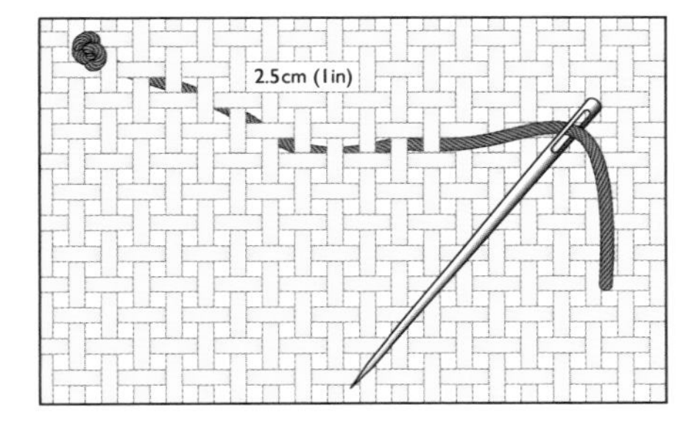

FINISHING STITCHING

At the back of the work, pass the needle and thread under several stitches and snip off the loose end close to the stitching. Begin new colours by passing the thread through stitches on the back in a similar way.

WORKING CROSS STITCH

Cross stitches can be worked singly or in two journeys but for neat stitching, keep the top stitch facing in the same direction. It does not matter which way it faces but it should be the same for the whole project.

Cross Stitch on Aida

Cross stitch on Aida fabric is normally worked over one block.

TO WORK A COMPLETE CROSS STITCH

Follow the numbered sequence in Fig 3: bring the needle up through the fabric at the bottom left corner, cross one block of the fabric and insert the needle at the top right corner. Push the needle through and bring it up at the bottom right corner, ready to complete the stitch in the top left corner. To work the adjacent stitch, bring the needle up at the bottom right-hand corner of the first stitch.

Fig 3 Single cross stitch on Aida

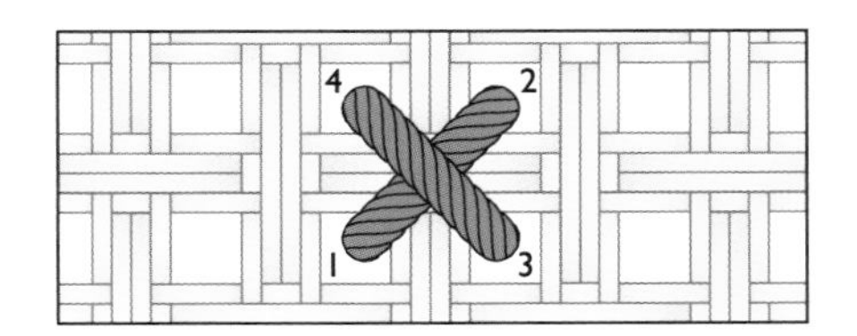

TO WORK CROSS STITCHES IN TWO JOURNEYS

Work the first leg of the cross stitch as above but instead of completing the stitch, work the adjacent half stitch and continue on to the end of the row (Fig 4). Complete all the crosses by working the other diagonals on the return journey.

Fig 4 Cross stitches worked in rows on Aida

Cross Stitch on Evenweave

Cross stitch on evenweave fabric is usually worked over two threads of the fabric in each direction, to even out any oddities in the thickness of the fibres. Follow the numbered sequence in Fig 5: bring the needle up through the fabric at the bottom left corner, cross two threads of the fabric up and to the right and then insert the needle at the top right corner. Push the needle through and bring it up at the bottom right corner, ready to complete the stitch in the top left corner.

Fig 5 Single cross stitch on evenweave

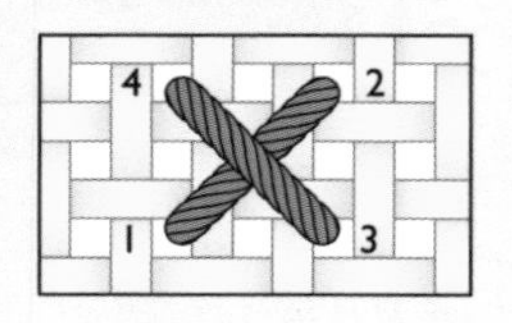

MAKING UP

You can make up your finished design in various ways and for the designs in this book framed pictures and cushions would work well. You may wish to block your finished stitching first, to ensure it is flat and right-angled. Use a steam iron carefully to press the embroidery into shape.

Making Up as a Framed Picture

You will need a picture frame with an aperture size to fit your cross stitch design, a piece of heavyweight card slightly smaller than the frame and some double-sided adhesive tape or fabric glue. Press the embroidery and centre it on the thick card. Fold the edges of the embroidery over the edges of the card and stick or glue it in place all round, making sure the stitching is taut and flat over the card. Place the embroidery into the frame and secure in place. You could omit the glass if you prefer.

Making Up as a Cushion

Press the embroidery and trim off excess fabric to within 1cm (⅜in) of the embroidery all round. Cut a piece of backing fabric the same size as the cushion front and place the pieces right sides together, aligning all the outer edges. Pin in place and then sew together all round using matching sewing thread and a 1cm (⅜in) seam, leaving a 15cm (6in) gap for turning through. Trim the corners a little, turn through to the right side and press the seam. Turn the edges of the gap under neatly and sew together with hand slipstitches.

Suppliers

Sew and So
www.sewandso.co.uk
For threads, needles and notions

Stitch Craft Create
www.stitchcraftcreate.co.uk
For fabrics and haberdashery

Hilary's Cross Stitch
www.hilaryscrossstitch.co.uk
For photo conversion cross stitch kits and original cross stitch designs

Acknowledgments

The publisher wishes to thank Linda Clements for writing the text and preparing the manuscript for this book, and Hilary Saxby for interpreting the Poldark images and preparing the charts and keys.

A DAVID & CHARLES BOOK

David & Charles is an imprint of F&W Media International, Ltd
Pynes Hill Court, Pynes Hill, Exeter, EX2 5AZ

F&W Media International, Ltd is a subsidiary of F+W Media, Inc
10151 Carver Road, Suite #200, Blue Ash, OH 45242, USA

First published in the UK in 2016

A catalogue record for this book is available from the British Library.

ISBN-13: 978-1-4463-0631-4 paperback
ISBN-10: 1-4463-0631-3 paperback

ISBN-13: 978-1-4463-7459-7 PDF
ISBN-10: 1-4463-7459-9 PDF

ISBN-13: 978-1-4463-7460-3 EPUB
ISBN-10: 1-4463-7460-2 EPUB

Printed in China by RR Donnelley for:
F&W Media International, Ltd
Pynes Hill Court, Pynes Hill, Exeter, EX2 5AZ

10 9 8 7 6 5 4 3 2 1

Acquisitions Editor: Sarah Callard
Desk Editor: Michelle Patten
Project Editor: Linda Clements
Art Editor: Anna Wade
Production Manager: Beverley Richardson

F+W Media publishes high quality books on a wide range of subjects.
For more great book ideas visit: www.stitchcraftcreate.co.uk

Layout of the digital edition of this book may vary depending on reader hardware and display settings.

Printed in Great Britain
by Amazon